❧ To ❧

❧ From ❧

101 Quick Tips
To Make Your Home
~ TASTE ~
SenseSational

Books by Terry Willits

101 Quick Tips to Make Your Home
Feel SenseSational

101 Quick Tips to Make Your Home
Look SenseSational

101 Quick Tips to Make Your Home
Smell SenseSational

101 Quick Tips to Make Your Home
Sound SenseSational

101 Quick Tips to Make Your Home
Taste SenseSational

Creating a SenseSational Home

If you are interested in having Terry Willits speak to your
church, organization, or special event, please contact:

InterAct Speaker's Bureau
8012 Brooks Chapel Road, Suite 243
Brentwood, Tennessee 37027
Telephone (800) 370-9932
Fax (615) 370-9939

101 QUICK TIPS
TO MAKE YOUR HOME
TASTE
SenseSational

TERRY WILLITS

ZondervanPublishingHouse

Grand Rapids, Michigan

A Division of HarperCollins*Publishers*

101 Quick Tips to Make Your Home Taste SenseSational
Copyright © 1996 by Terry Willits

Requests for information should be addressed to:

ZondervanPublishingHouse
Grand Rapids, Michigan 49530

Library of Congress Cataloging-in-Publication Data

Willits, Terry, 1959–
       101 quick tips to make your home taste SenseSational / Terry Willits.
       p.   cm.
       ISBN: 0-310-20226-4
       1. Cookery.   2. Food.   3. Christian life.   I. Title.
    TX651.W55   1996
    641.3—dc20   96-13342
                                                                                  CIP

This edition printed on acid-free paper and meets the American National Standards
Institute Z39.48 standard.

Edited by Rachel Boers
Interior Illustrations by Edsel Arnold
Interior design by Sherri Hoffman

Printed in the United States of America

96 97 98 99 00 01 02 /❖ QF/ 10 9 8 7 6 5 4 3 2 1

For he satisfies the thirsty and fills

the hungry with good things.

Psalm 107:9

Introduction

— ⚜ —

God has blessed us with bountiful food and drink to nourish our bodies and satisfy our taste buds. In the same way, we can bless our family, friends, and ourselves by preparing healthy, delicious food and beverages in our homes.

God has given us almost ten thousand taste buds. Every taste of the food he has created for us gives us the chance to relish something delectable. Yet with the busyness of life, it seems we seldom slow down to savor the flavors of food and enjoy them with grateful hearts.

May the following tips inspire you to fill your home with life and love as you fill it with God's abundant bounty. Keep in mind, some of the most pleasing foods and drinks are also the most simple. Have fun tantalizing the taste buds in your home!

terry.

101 Quick Tips
To Make Your Home
❧ TASTE ❧
SenseSational

Celebrate his bounty.

God has blessed us with an abundance of delicious natural foods to strengthen, sustain, and satisfy. The vast variety of colors, textures, shapes, and flavors of food demonstrate his goodness to us. Honor God and your family by filling your home and your body with healthy, tasty foods he has created.

2

Put function first.

*O*rganize your kitchen so that it is a comfortable and enjoyable place in which to cook and prepare food. Keep quality kitchen equipment and utensils that make kitchen tasks easier, and give away unneeded items. Arrange cabinet and drawer contents in a way that is convenient for tasks carried out nearby.

3

Live and learn.

When we stop learning, we stop living. Plan to become a better cook each year. Ask God to help make cooking a fun and interesting job for you. Learn more about nutrition. Take a cooking course with a friend. Try at least one new recipe a month to help cultivate new tastes.

4

Eat a variety of foods.

*H*aving a variety of foods to choose from makes it more interesting to cook, serve, and eat. Variety also contributes to a sense of satisfaction that prevents overeating. And eating different, delicious, healthy foods assures our bodies get the nutrients they need. Plan a variety of menus, using cookbooks and magazines for inspiration.

Satisfy simply.

$\mathcal{K}$eep foods and menus simple —
they will be healthier, and you will be better
able to enjoy the food's natural flavor. Usually,
the fewer ingredients a recipe or menu has, the
cheaper and easier it will be to prepare. A
healthy piece of meat, a salad, and a whole-
grain bread make a superb simple meal.

6

Get ready for market.

*K*eep an ongoing grocery list in your kitchen. Jot down items on the list when they get low or as family members make food requests. To keep shelves well-stocked and to prevent being caught without a needed staple, double-check your refrigerator and pantry before going to the grocery store.

Plan your menus.

You will waste less food and save time and money while shopping if you plan your menus in advance. Plan meals that are quick to prepare or can be served more than once. Hang a list in your kitchen of menu options, crossing menus off after they have been served.

8

Shop wisely.

*B*e a wise steward with your food funds. Clip coupons. Skim the Sunday newspaper for special prices on grocery items. Stock up on nonperishable items when they are on sale. Eat a snack or meal before shopping to prevent overbuying.

Get back to basics.

When planning meals and shopping, keep in mind the four basic food groups and daily servings needed for healthy eating: 2–3 servings of milk/dairy products; 3–5 servings of vegetables; 2–4 servings of fruit; 6–11 servings of bread, cereal, rice, and pasta; 2–3 servings of beef, poultry, fish, eggs, and beans.

10

Stock up on healthy foods.

When we eat properly, we feel and look our best — it's how God designed our bodies to work. Make the most of the life he has given you by eating healthy. The closer foods are to their natural source, the better they are for you. Stock up on healthy foods so that when hunger hits, you'll reach for the right things.

Begin with breakfast.

*S*tarting your day out with breakfast will jump-start your digestive system into working efficiently throughout the day. It can be as simple as a glass of fresh fruit juice and a banana, a muffin, a bagel, or yogurt topped with granola.

12

Find the freshest.

*W*hen preparing foods, start with the freshest ingredients possible. This assures the best flavor and most nutritious content. Find a local farmer's market or produce stand and frequent it for fresh, seasonal produce. Avoid produce in plastic wrap; it will most likely not have as much flavor.

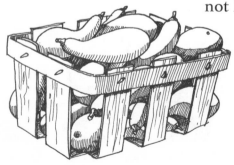

Relish your refrigerator.

*D*isplay foods attractively inside your refrigerator. Use clear glass or plastic food containers to store foods. Place fruits and vegetables in bowls. Enclose meats and cheeses in clear plastic bags. Food that is out of sight is out of mind, and will probably spoil before it's remembered.

14

Celebrate the seasons.

*F*or the fullest flavors, serve food and beverages that celebrate each season's bounty. To know what is in season, look for what is plentiful, healthy looking, and reasonably priced. Cool months call for hot apple cider, pot roast, citrus fruits, or vegetable soup. Warmer months welcome fresh lemonade, corn on the cob, melons, or sliced tomatoes.

15

Keep recipes current.

*C*lean out recipes you won't ever use, and plan to try those you keep. Collect good and easy recipes from outstanding cooks you know. Have a few favorite cookbooks with healthy, quick recipes. Mark recipes that are winners. Browse through a cookbook in bed at night for cooking inspiration.

16

Share a specialty.

Find a food you enjoy cooking, and make it your trademark dish: homemade breads, cookies, soups, salads — whatever comes easy and is enjoyable to you. Share your specialty with others.

17

Let little hands help.

*T*hough letting children help with the cooking may not be the fastest method, your efforts may bear rich fruit. Children are more apt to experiment with eating if they have helped in preparation, and cooking together allows you to talk with them while they help.

18

Freeze it!

*F*reezing is one of the best ways to preserve flavor, but even frozen food doesn't last forever. Store foods in moisture-proof packaging like plastic containers, freezer bags, or heavy foil. Mark contents and the date frozen clearly on packages. Eat cooked frozen foods within six weeks to assure freshest flavor.

19

Triple the taste.

Cook a triple batch of a recipe. Eat one, freeze one, and share one with a family or neighbor in need of encouragement. You will not only get two great meals for your family, you'll feel the joy of sharing! (If you have children, let them help deliver the food, so they can learn the joy of sharing too!)

20

Go with garlic.

Garlic gives great flavor to foods. To prevent them from drying out, skin cloves and refrigerate them in a jar of olive oil. You can use cloves as needed for garlic-flavored cooking oil or salad dressing. Prepeeled or minced garlic is available in most grocery stores. For a great garlic taste, rub a prepeeled clove inside a wooden salad bowl before adding greens.

21

Pep it up with pepper.

*P*epper adds spice, texture, and eye appeal to almost any food. It loses its potent flavor soon after it is ground, so for the fullest flavor, grind your own fresh peppercorns with a pepper mill. Try crushing peppercorns in a paper bag to coat steaks, a roast, or fish before cooking. Or simmer whole peppercorns in slow-cooking dishes.

22

Make it better with butter.

*B*utter always adds a burst of rich flavor. For a terrific taste, flavor butter by sprinkling jalapeno, onion, black pepper, basil, and parsley onto a stick of softened butter. Mix all the ingredients together, roll them into a log, wrap, and freeze for use on broiled meats and fish or to stir into vegetables or pastas. You can also mix fruit preserves and a touch of confectioners' sugar with softened butter for fresh breads.

Flavor with fresh herbs.

*F*resh herbs, available in most grocery produce sections, help accent the natural flavor of any food. Try using fresh herbs for garnishes or in salads. Mix whole leaves of basil, cilantro, or mint with salad greens. (Dried herbs are much more potent in flavor than fresh herbs, so use one-third as much dried herbs than fresh when cooking.)

24

Vary your vinegars.

*V*inegars give vitality to many dishes, with few calories and no fat. They come in a variety of flavors and colors. Tantalize your taste buds by experimenting with different ones. For a somewhat sweet flavor, try rice or raspberry vinegar in green salads with fruit. For a tangy taste, use tarragon, balsamic, or red wine vinegar in salads with vegetables.

Dress up your salad.

Make sure greens are dry before dressing a salad. Test different dressings and oils for flavor. For a tasty dressing, add Dijon mustard to oil and vinegar. Or for a citrus zing, replace vinegar with the juice of a freshly squeezed lemon, lime, or orange. A dressing should enhance the salad's flavor, not overpower it. After mixing a dressing, toss it well and taste it before serving.

26

Choose the "cream of the crop."

For maximum freshness and vitamin content, choose vegetables with rich, bright colors that are firm to the touch: the darker and richer the color, the greater the nutrients. Smaller vegetables often have a more tender texture and more flavor. Steam fresh vegetables lightly in water with lemon juice to keep nutrients and vibrant color.

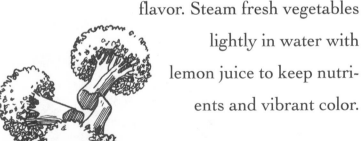

Consider carrots.

Carrots are a versatile kitchen staple, available year-round. Buy a bag of prepeeled, miniature carrots to have on hand for a ready-to-eat, healthy, crunchy snack. Add chopped carrots to soups, stews, and tomato sauce for a natural and nutritious sweet flavor. For a superb side dish, lightly sauté carrots in butter, brown sugar, orange juice, and basil.

28

Serve artichokes as appetizers.

Spring is prime time for artichokes. Purchase artichokes that are heavy and have tightly closed leaves. To keep their vibrant color, steam them in water with lemon juice. The artichoke is ready when its cooked leaves

lift easily from its base. Dip artichoke leaves and heart in lemon butter or mayonnaise mixed with parmesan cheese.

Pile on the potatoes.

The potato is the most consumed vegetable in America today. Be creative with this economical vegetable. Serve potatoes hot or cold, as a side dish, in a salad, or as a main dish. Load a baked potato with fresh vegetables for a healthy meal. Celebrate spring with new potatoes steamed in butter and black pepper, and tossed in fresh dill.

30

Scoop it out.

A natural serving container makes a creative edible dish for delicious foods. Hollow out a loaf of bread or a small cabbage head for vegetable dips. Fill a large beefsteak tomato with chicken, tuna, or shrimp salad. Stuff and cook a green pepper with ground beef and rice.

31

On with the onions!

$\mathcal{E}$xperiment with different flavored onions. Add leeks to soup broth for a mild, somewhat sweet taste. Use fresh, frozen, or dried chives in baked potatoes and egg or seafood dishes to bring color and a delicate onion flavor. Slice red onions to enhance salads and sandwiches. Bake sweet onions, like Vidalias, whole in butter for a tasty side dish. Try raw scallions in dip.

32

Tempt with tomatoes.

Take advantage of tasty tomatoes in the summer. Eat a plum tomato whole like an apple, slice it for sandwiches, or puree it for sauce. Serve sliced beefsteak tomatoes with chopped parsley for a simple summer vegetable. Lightly sauté cherry tomatoes in olive oil and season them to taste with fresh ground pepper and salt. To assure the fullest flavor, avoid using tomatoes out of season.

Cool off with cucumbers.

*F*or a cool summer side dish, marinate cucumber slices and red onions in cider vinegar, water, salt, and pepper. For a healthy snack, munch on crunchy, raw pickling cucumbers.

34

Satisfy with squash.

*E*njoy the succulent tastes of seasonal squash. In the fall and winter, slice acorn squash in half, remove seeds and steam it with butter, brown sugar, and cracked peppercorns. In the spring and summer, stir fry, steam, or grill yellow crookneck and green zucchini squash. As an exquisite side dish, sauté miniature squash in butter and spices. Or eat squash raw with dips.

Munch on mushrooms.

Mushrooms are good all year long in salads, egg dishes, or sauces. Sauté whole or sliced mushrooms in burgundy or white cooking wine for a delicious topping for beef, poultry, or fish or as a side dish. Fill hollowed-out mushroom caps with chopped spinach, garlic, and grated Parmesan cheese. Broil the caps until the filling is slightly crunchy. Serve as an appetizer or side dish.

36

Bring on the berries!

Enjoy delicious berries when in season. Luscious berries should be plump, vibrantly colored, and unblemished. Avoid overripe berries that are leaking juice and strawberries with brown leaves. Serve berries plain, with a touch of cream or whipped cream, in salads or cereals. For a healthy, all-fruit spread, try berry preserves on toast, bagels, or croissants.

Freeze fruit.

*F*reeze fresh seedless grapes for a cold, sweet snack. Enjoy all-natural frozen fruit juice bars in raspberry, strawberry, or grape. You can make your own by freezing fresh fruit juice in small paper cups. For a handle, insert a wooden popsicle stick just before the juice freezes. Peel away the cup when ready to eat.

38

Guarantee great grapes.

Gently shake a bunch of grapes before buying. Fresh, sweet grapes should cling tightly to the stem, and sour grapes often have a brown or grayish color. Eat grapes for a healthy snack or toss them into salads for color, texture, and flavor. For an easy meal, serve a bunch of grapes with a wedge of cheese and French bread.

Reach for the ripe.

The ripeness of fruits such as peaches, plums, pears, and nectarines can be tested by placing them in your palm and gently squeezing them. If the fruit gives to light pressure and smells sweet and delicious, it's ready to eat. For the juiciest citrus fruits, select those that are the heaviest. To ripen fruit quickly, place it in a brown paper bag, close the bag loosely, and store it at room temperature.

40

Maximize your salads.

 $\mathcal{S}$ alads are an easy, delicious way to eat more fruits and vegetables throughout the day. Keep salads healthy with low-fat ingredients like fruits and vegetables, kidney or garbanzo beans, and lean beef, poultry, or seafood.

Go for fresh greens.

*B*uild salads with a tasty mixture of leafy greens. The darker the greens, the greater the nutrients. Combine tangy greens with those milder in flavor, crisp greens with tender varieties, and pale greens with those flashier in color. If you wash and wrap fresh greens in paper towel as soon as you get them home, they'll be convenient and clean when you want to whip up a salad.

42

Fix a quick salad.

*B*uy packages of ready-to-use spinach, lettuces, and slaw mixes; they cost only a few pennies more and are very convenient. Choose packages carefully to assure freshness. For an instant salad, cut a wedge of iceberg lettuce and drizzle on your favorite healthy dressing.

Go nuts!

Enhance salads with a handful of nuts or sunflower seeds. Try walnuts, pecans, almonds, or peanuts in salads, toasting them lightly to bring out their flavor. If you don't have young children in your home, place a wooden bowl filled with different sizes, shapes, and flavors of nuts in your living room. Leave a nutcracker and a pick in the bowl so family and friends can help themselves.

44

Liven up with olives.

*A*dding black olives is a fast and flavorful way to enhance many dishes like antipastos, pizzas, salads, chicken, spaghetti, and casseroles. Save time by buying them prepared as you need them — sliced, chopped, whole with pits, or pitted. Green olives are delicious in salads as well.

Try turkey.

*F*or healthy, low-fat protein, roast a whole turkey, turkey breast, or boneless turkey breast. Gobble on it for a few days; then make turkey and rice soup. Use ground turkey instead of, or combined with, ground beef. Keep sliced deli turkey on hand for sandwiches and salads. For a fun change, try tasty turkey salami for sandwiches.

46

Bake bread.

*B*read can add sustenance, flavor, and most importantly, fiber to any meal. Breads made from whole grains are the best for our bodies. Enjoy a banana bran muffin for breakfast, a simple sandwich on whole wheat bread for lunch, or a whole grain roll with dinner.

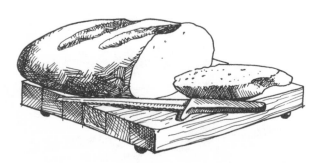

47

Pork out.

*P*ork and fruit are a natural pair. Simmer cutlets in your favorite jam mixed with a little vinegar or water. For a sweet and sour taste, microwave pork with pineapple and green pepper in French dressing, orange marmalade, and dry onion soup mix. For delicious, flavorful meat, grill a marinated pork roast or tenderloin.

48

Please pass the pasta!

*P*repare various sizes, shapes, colors, and flavors of pastas. Sauté fresh vegetables in garlic and olive oil and toss them in cooked pasta. Add tuna, chicken, or shrimp, if desired, and serve piping hot or chilled. For an easy seafood pasta dish, steam fresh shrimp or mussels and place them on spaghetti that's been tossed in a red clam sauce.

Simmer soups.

$\mathcal{L}$earn to master at least one easy soup. Try a hot favorite, like French onion soup, in the winter, or a cool, vegetable-rich gazpacho in the summer. Buy cans of healthy soups for convenient, quick meals. For an easy and hearty meal, serve soup, salad, and fresh bread, or soup and a sandwich.

50

Go healthy with snack attacks.

Have healthy snacks on hand when hunger hits. Try fresh or dried fruits, pretzels, nuts, raisins, popcorn, or vegetables cut up in cold water. Sprinkle popcorn with Parmesan cheese. Buy baked tortilla chips instead of fried, and serve with salsa. Set out a light snack when others come home at the end of the day.

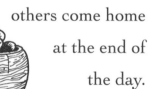

Have fun with food!

*B*reak out of the mold of boring mealtimes. Have an indoor picnic, or a make-your-own pizza, tostada, or fajita party. Try a pasta or potato bar. Let kids pitch in on the fun! Make a ritual of certain meals, like celebrating the weekend with a fun meal on Friday night or a big breakfast on Satur-day morning.

52

Get fancy with fruit.

*M*ake a delightful dessert by jazzing up crepes, waffles, pancakes, pastry puffs, angel food cake, or shortcake with fresh fruit and ice cream or whipped cream. Try timesaving, ready-made crepes, cakes, frozen waffles, or pastry puffs. For an extra-tasty surprise, use strawberry or chocolate flavored whipped creams, available in most dairy departments.

Order up an omelet.

Omelets are a quick and easy meal to serve for breakfast, lunch, or dinner. Use the freshest eggs and ingredients possible. For a fluffy omelet, use eggs that are room temperature. Toss in your favorite vegetables, cheese, or meat for a marvelous meal anytime.

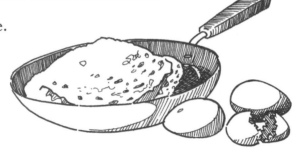

54

Say cheese.

The taste of rich cheese melts in your mouth. Serve French bread with warm Brie cheese topped with sliced almonds. Mix cream cheese with minced garlic and coarse ground pepper for a tasty spread on celery sticks or crackers. Crumble blue cheese, apple slices, and walnuts into a spinach salad. Add Feta cheese to peppers, ripe olives, and greens for a Greek salad.

55

Go for it!

*F*or a "too-tired-to-cook" night, pick up a healthy dinner at a specialty food shop or order in Chinese. Try to make it the exception, not the rule. Thank God for providing your meal and enjoy a night off!

56

Set the stage.

A set table sends a message of care and preparation. The most enjoyable meals are prepared simply and presented beautifully. Even if eating alone, value the life God has created in you by setting a pretty place setting for yourself. Food always tastes

better when there

is beauty to

behold.

Calm with candlelight.

*L*ight a candle when you sit down to dinner. The quiet flicker of the flame will calm you so that you eat and digest your food more slowly and linger over your meal. Eating should be an experience that causes you to not only stop and savor the tastes God has created, but to savor life itself.

58

Have a seat.

$\mathcal{M}$ake it an important habit to sit when eating meals — it will affect your mind-set and your meal. Also, eat with others whenever possible. A meal shared with family or friends is ultimately a more satisfying experience. A person is more likely to eat healthy when dining with others. If you live alone, why not start a supper club and take turns cooking?

Cleanse your palette.

Serve a small scoop of lemon or lime sherbet as a light, refreshing dessert or palette cleanser between courses. To freshen breath after meals, eat a sprig of parsley or mint. Place a jar of peppermints where you exit your home for a quick breath of freshness when walking out the door.

60

Feast your eyes on food.

*T*antalize your taste buds by serving food attractively. Think of your plate as a canvas and your food as the painting. For example, rather than toss a mixture of fruits into a bowl, arrange them beautifully as a fruit platter. When planning menus, vary color, texture, and taste for an appealing meal.

61

Celebrate life!

*F*or a special celebration or birthday meal, allow the person being honored to select the menu. Serve their favorite food on a "You are special today" plate or any sentimental piece of dishware. If you have china, silver, and crystal, enjoy them frequently instead of saving them for special occasions.

62

Gussy up with garnishes.

Garnishes are to food what accessories are to furniture. Observe how restaurants display foods and accent with garnishes. Fresh fruit, flowers, vegetables, and lettuce leaves all make good garnishes. You can also use fresh parsley or mint sprigs for a touch of green garnish to meals.

63

Cleanse your body, soul, and mind.

Consider fasting to draw you closer to God in prayer and cleanse your body of impurities. While you fast, be sure to drink plenty of pure drinking water. After fasting, you will feel better, have a renewed intimacy with God, and better appreciate the simple pleasure of taste and eating.

64

Skewer it.

Skewer tasty, colorful combinations of food. On metal skewers, grill beef, shrimp, or chicken with mushrooms, onions, cherry tomatoes, and green peppers.

Create an edible centerpiece.

*F*or a beautiful and economical focal point, create an edible centerpiece. Fill a basket or bowl with colorful, seasonal, fresh fruit or vegetables. Use squash and small pumpkins in the fall, green or red apples in the winter, lemons and limes in the spring, peaches, plums, and pears in the summer.

66

Be a happy hostess.

When practicing hospitality, keep it simple and easy by preparing as much ahead of time as possible. Serve a simple casserole, salad, and bread. Food should never be more important than the people. The more relaxed you are, the more relaxed everyone will be. Preparing ahead will help you enjoy your family and friends and make your time together casual and comfortable.

67

Try a trifle.

*C*reate your own sweet, layered luxury. Use a large, clear glass bowl, and alternate layers of your favorite sweet treats like unfrosted cake cubes, fruit, pudding, whipped cream, and chocolate bar bits. Drizzle with a generous portion of chocolate sauce or thawed frozen strawberries in their juice. Refrigerate overnight to allow ingredients to congeal.

68

Go bananas!

*F*or a scrumptious, inexpensive dessert to warm your heart and stomach, make bananas Foster. Slice bananas lengthwise, then melt butter, brown sugar, and cinnamon and pour the mixture over the bananas. Add coconut, if desired. Sauté on the stove or bake in the oven. Serve hot on top of vanilla ice cream for a great winter dessert.

Create colossal cookies.

*U*se an ice cream scooper to portion out a batch of your favorite cookie dough. Wet your hands with water and smash the dough down into five-inch rounds on greased cookie sheets. After baking, write out a message in frosting to a loved one.

70

Toast your taste buds.

*M*ake a dessert treat that is not only tasty, but toasty too! Bake brownies and serve them while still hot topped with vanilla ice cream or yogurt. For an instant and sweet frosting for cupcakes or any baked goods, top them with marshmallows two minutes before removing the baked item from the oven.

71

Fix fresh fruit.

*F*resh in-season fruit is a terrific dessert alternative to heavy, sweet desserts. Dish out juicy peaches and cream, sweet chunks of watermelon with mint leaves, or succulent strawberries with tender slices of peeled kiwi. Combine honeydew balls, blueberries, and green grapes, and toss them in lime juice with fresh mint leaves.

72

Dip it.

*F*or a fun dessert sure to tantalize the taste buds, dip fresh fruits on toothpicks into brown sugar, powdered sugar, coconut, yogurt, and caramel or fruit sauce (available in most produce sections). Enjoy apple slices covered in warm caramel sauce. Dip bananas in chocolate sauce, then in coconut. Savor strawberries dipped in vanilla yogurt, then in brown sugar.

73

Cover it.

To cover strawberries, dried fruits, caramel, nuts, or pretzels with chocolate, cut up your favorite semisweet or sweet bar of chocolate or white chocolate, melting the pieces over very low heat in a small, heavy pan. Fruit must be thoroughly dried before dipping or the chocolate will not stick. Use a toothpick to hold food while dipping.

74

Scream for ice cream.

*F*or an impressive but easy and inexpensive dessert, layer ice cream sandwiches in a flat pan, top with Cool Whip, then with Heath Bar bits. Repeat layers. Freeze. Before serving, remove from freezer, cut in squares, and drizzle with hot fudge sauce. Your guests will never guess how easy it was to prepare!

Fondue for fun.

*F*or a fun, interactive way to prepare and enjoy food, serve fondue. Start with cheese fondue with breads and vegetables as an appetizer. For dinner, try cooking chicken, shrimp, or beef in peanut oil, and serve with tasty side sauces. For dessert, dip fresh fruits or cakes in warm chocolate sauce.

76

Eat outdoors.

*E*njoy the spectacular sights, sounds, and smells of nature by eating outdoors. When spring is in the air, serve a leisurely weekend breakfast outdoors, or sit outdoors and sip a cup of tea while you spend time with God. On a sunny afternoon, put on your bathing suit and eat a picnic lunch in your backyard. On a beautiful evening, dine by candlelight under the stars.

Grill for goodness.

If you have a grill, use it often for tasty, quick meals and an easy, no pots or pans clean-up. Gas grill smoking chips bring the smoky flavors of hickory and mesquite to outdoor barbecuing. Add butter, salt, and pepper to corn on the cob, potatoes, whole onions, or squash, cover them in heavy foil, and toss them on the grill while your meat cooks.

78

Make it marvelous with marinade.

Delicious marinades add flavor and interest to grilling. Marinate salmon or tuna in teriyaki sauce and lime juice before grilling. Baste often while cooking. Tenderize a flank steak in Italian dressing before grilling. Marinate chicken in Dijon mustard or soy sauce and cook on foil on the grill. Baste shrimp or fish with lemon butter and pepper.

Feast on finger foods.

Enjoy the occasional casual pleasure of eating foods that invite you to roll up your sleeves and dig in. Serve corn on the cob, barbecue ribs, crabs, chicken, peel and eat shrimp, or wedges of watermelon. The more senses we use, the more memories we retain. Finger foods make memorable meals. The outdoors is an ideal setting for a fun finger feast.

80

Bring out the baskets.

$\mathcal{U}$se baskets as attractive containers for serving food. Use flat baskets to hold hot casserole dishes, and baskets lined with pretty napkins to serve chips and breads. Try a small basket lined with a paper doily to hold a sandwich, fresh vegetables, and a pickle for a lunch that's quick to clean up.

Master one menu.

$\mathcal{I}$f you don't feel confident when it comes to cooking for company, come up with one great menu you can serve whenever you have guests. Master it by making it often. Enjoy your company as they enjoy your delicious "specialty."

82

Grow a garden.

*I*f you have a sunny spot in your backyard and the slightest urge to try to grow something, dig in. Plant one little tomato or herb plant and see what happens. What do

you have to lose? A little time and water may breed tasty rewards.

Offer a gracious greeting.

*O*ffering and preparing a beverage for a family member or friend is a warm and gracious gesture that says "welcome." Keep a variety of beverages on hand to satisfy the slightest thirst. Make it a ritual to prepare a healthy, tasty beverage for yourself when you come home.

84

Drink water.

Retrain your taste buds to enjoy the fresh taste of pure drinking water. The more you drink, the better you'll feel! If your tap water isn't tasty and you don't have a water filter, buy drinking water. Keep a cold pitcher of it in the refrigerator, and place a small carafe of water with a glass by your bedside.

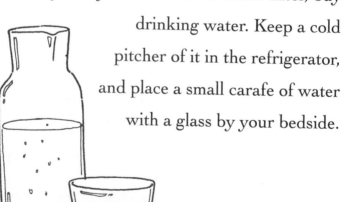

Sip some cider.

*E*njoy the sweet taste of fresh apple cider in the fall. Serve it cold or hot. For a quick and inexpensive alternative to apple cider, melt one cup of red hot cinnamon candies in one gallon of apple juice. It's a great beverage for parties or to make ahead and microwave one cup at a time.

86

Pour in the punch.

For a delicious, refreshing punch that won't stain if spilled, add lemon-lime carbonated drink to white grape or apple juice. Serve over crushed ice with a mint leaf.

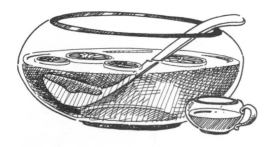

Quench your thirst.

Keep plenty of chilled, fresh fruit juices to quench the thirst of those you love. Try orange, grapefruit, apple, and grape juice, as well as many fruit combinations. For a fun afternoon with children that will teach them to enjoy serving others, set up a lemonade stand in your neighborhood. Don't charge for the lemonade. The experience will be priceless.

88

Let the sunshine in.

Make iced tea the easy way — let the warm sunshine brew it! Place fresh water and tea bags in a loosely lidded glass jar and set it in the sun. Let the tea bags steep for several hours. Stir in fresh mint and sugar, if desired, and refrigerate. For a refreshing taste, add fresh orange juice or lemonade to iced tea.

Top off your hot chocolate.

*E*nhance a steamy mug of hot chocolate with a tasty swirl of whipped cream and a sprinkle of cinnamon sugar or chocolate shavings. At Christmas, add a candy cane stir stick. For a cool hot chocolate sundae, add a small scoop of vanilla or chocolate ice cream and top it with small marshmallows, sprinkles, and a maraschino cherry.

90

Brew a cup of coffee.

Store ground coffee and coffee beans in airtight containers. Coffee should stay fresh for two to three weeks in the refrigerator and for about two months in the freezer. Defrost beans before grinding. When brewing, start with cold water, preferably filtered drinking water. Transfer freshly-brewed coffee to an airtight, thermal carafe to keep it from tasting burnt or bitter.

Create a zesty zing.

*B*ring citrus flavor to any beverage by squeezing in a lemon, lime, or orange, leaving the fruit in the glass to garnish the beverage. Add lemon or lime to water or sodas. Give hot tea a zingy twist by adding an orange peel to the teapot a few minutes before serving tea.

92

Trim the rim.

*T*here are many ways to add a beautiful touch of taste to a beverage. Stir tea, coffee, or hot chocolate with a cinnamon stick. Garnish tomato juice with a leafy stalk of celery. Add mint to lemonade or fruit juice. Slide a whole strawberry or an orange or lemon slice onto a glass rim. For a sweet luxury to the lips, wet the rim of a glass and touch it to a plate of sugar. After freezing the glass, fill it with ice and your favorite sweet beverage.

Stir in some sugar.

*D*ispense sugar cubes into your beverage with tongs, or add a small amount of sugar by using a sugar pourer with a lidded spout. For a sweet holiday treat, mix granulated sugar with colored sugar crystals.

94

Give a new twist to ice cubes.

*F*ill an ice tray one-third full with water or another beverage, such as lemonade or tea. Then place a mint leaf, citrus peel, raspberry, or an edible flower, like a pansy, in each compartment. When slightly frozen, fill the ice tray to the top with liquid and freeze.

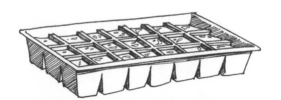

Eat where you live.

*O*ne of the easiest ways to bring variety and pleasure to the foods we eat is to change the room setting. Take advantage of cozy fires on cold winter nights, sit on the floor at your coffee table, use wicker lap trays or television trays, or eat at a card table.

96

Savor the flavor.

Set an atmosphere that will enhance your enjoyment of a tasty meal by turning off any distractions. The eating environment needs to be as calming as possible. If it is stressful, it will affect your digestion process and prevent you from fully enjoying the flavor of the food.

97

Take time for tea.

Whether alone or with a friend or family member, enjoy the simple and satisfying ritual of taking time out of your day to drink a cup of hot tea. Try several different flavored tea bags or add a touch of cream to tea for rich flavor. Keep a tin of sugar cookies on hand to eat when having tea; they store well and keep fresh. Invite neighborhood children to a dress-up tea party.

98

Treat with a little sweet.

*F*ill a pretty jar with special, tasty candies that coordinate with your decor. Tuck some snack-size candy bars in the freezer for an occasional sweet surprise. Or, as a real splurge in sweetness, tantalize the taste buds like the finest hotels do: Fold down the

bedsheets of a house-guest or loved one and place a tasty bite of something sweet on their pillow.

Enjoy the lap
of luxury.

*T*reat a loved one or yourself to a meal or snack in bed for a celebration, a sickness, or just for a taste of encouragement. Use a wicker bed tray or a serving tray. To start their school year out with an extra measure of homegrown love, serve kids breakfast in bed on their first day of class.

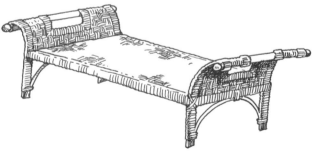

100

Sip yourself to sleep.

After an especially stressful day or when having difficulty sleeping, treat yourself or a loved one to a cup of hot tea in bed. Herbal tea is naturally decaffeinated, and the soothing flavor will quiet your body and mind. Try chamomile for a subtle, relaxing taste.

Taste and see that the Lord is good.

*C*hrist is the true Bread of Life. While delicious food may temporarily meet our physical needs, only Jesus Christ can feed our spirits and satisfy us fully. Spend time getting to know the Savior who fully satisfies.

More from Terry Willits ...

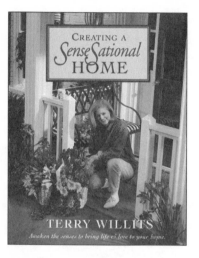

Creating a SenseSational Home is the complete guide to discover how awakening the five senses of sight, smell, taste, touch, and sound can create an atmosphere of love and cheer. From warmly-lit entrances that welcome family and friends to comfortable, homey interiors that invite them to stay and unwind . . . from fragrant bouquets to the tranquil ticking of a clock . . . *Creating a SenseSational Home* shows you simple and affordable ways to turn your home into a relaxing, inviting, and refreshing environment.

ISBN 0-310-20223-X
$19.99

ZondervanPublishingHouse
Grand Rapids, Michigan
http://www.zondervan.com

A Division of HarperCollins*Publishers*

America Online
AOL Keyword:zon